The Should Stick

Stop being a people pleaser. It's time to be you.

By Tracey Hartshorn
Illustrated by Matt Roberts

First Published in Great Britain by IW Press Ltd 2022

Copyright © 2022 Tracey Hartshorn

Tracey Hartshorn asserts her right to be identified as the author of this work in accordance with the Copyright, Designs and Patents Act 1988

Front cover illustration and interior illustrations by Matt Roberts © 2022

Interior formatting and cover graphic design by 18 Design Ltd

All rights reserved.

No part of this publication may be reproduced, stored or transmitted without the expression permission, in writing, from the author.

ISBN-13: 978-1-8383330-2-7 (paperback)

IW Press Ltd, 62-64 Market Street, Ashby de la Zouch, LE65 1AN

www.iliffe-wood.co.uk

For Marcus and Glenn

Contents

Words from the Author — i

Part One
The Should Stick — 1

Part Two
What Next? — 47

Part Three
How to Be Me – The Labels Exercise — 55

Acknowledgements — 87

About Tracey Hartshorn — 89

About Matt Roberts — 90

Words from the Author
Your transformation starts here

This book will change your life – if you let it.

The process will change you – if you're open to it.

The results will be life changing – if you want it.

You're someone who has very little time for yourself. You focus so much on others, that you are lost and unseen. You offer your ear to others but are left waiting to be listened to.

You're pulled in different directions, as you try to please everyone around you.

You're fed up with being told what to do.

Your life is full. Full of doing everything for everyone else, and nothing for yourself. You are not just second you are last in every queue.

You would like a different life. A life where you can state your needs and have them met. A life where you feel happy, fulfilled, and able to focus on yourself. Where the needs of others take second place, as your needs move to the front of the queue. A life where your dreams can come true.

To achieve lasting change in your life, you need a place to start. The Should Stick is that starting point.

The story is simple, the concepts behind it are not. The journey to authenticity can be long. No book can describe the whole route, nor can it predict the exact outcomes. By its very nature, achieving authenticity requires a unique journey which only you can design. That doesn't mean there aren't some shortcuts and navigational aids.

I bring my training and experience, as a coach and psychotherapist, to support you with this process. I've worked with hundreds of people, to help them achieve the life they want to live.

For myself, I work on me every day. It's like the most complex jigsaw, and it's the most important puzzle there is. The result of the work is that I am more complete; there are fewer pieces missing, and I've got all the sides and corners in position. I also really like the picture.

The Should Stick is my story and I offer it as inspiration to start your own life changing journey back to YOU.

Part One

The Should Stick

This is me.

I am unique and amazing.

I feel awesome because I know who I am and I choose to be me.

That makes me happy.

It's great to be me but...

I didn't always feel like this.

I want to tell you a story about how I got here...

Grab yourself a mug of something tasty and I'll begin.

My story involves a "Should Stick".

When I was born, I was me.
There really was nothing
else I needed to be.

I was happy just
being me.

I was 4 years old when I saw my first Should Stick. I think they'd always been there but I was so focussed on being me, I hadn't paid much attention to them.

When people started to prod me with their Should Sticks, my life changed.

I wasn't very happy at being prodded but it looked like this was how life was meant to be.

It looked like I ought to have a Should Stick too and...

...one appeared in my hand.

I learned to use the stick with other people.

Sometimes it was a gentle poke.

"You should...."

Sometimes I poked too hard.

"YOU SHOULD..."

My Should Stick was easy to hold, easy to carry, and easy to use. I didn't feel right without it.

I decided to take it with me everywhere.

I started to use the Should Stick on myself.

It hurt.

I told myself 'I should stop' but this seemed to make it worse.

Sometimes it felt like the Should Stick was good for me.

Other times it felt bad for me.

I used the Should Stick on other people.

"You should be happy."

"You shouldn't cry."

When I did that, the Should Stick made me feel things.

It made me feel powerful.

It made me feel happy.

It made me laugh.

It made me feel proud.

It made me feel sad.

It made me feel guilty.

The Should Stick made the people I poked feel the same.

Other people had Should Sticks and they poked me...

...I didn't like it.

Some days all we did to each other was...

poke "You should...."

poke "You should...."

poke "You should...."

poke "You should...."

Sometimes I tried to leave the Should Stick at home.

But it didn't like to be left behind.

Somehow it always found me and I ended up poking someone when I didn't want to.

I wondered if the Should Stick was more in control of me than I was of it.

I wanted to get rid of my Should Stick
but it's named quite well.

Every time I said 'I should get rid of you' it
got even stickier. With every *poke* and every
should it stuck more and more.

Sometimes my life was one big...

I was so full of *shoulds*, I couldn't remember what it was like to be me.

I remembered my younger self and how happy I was.

Life was simple without the Should Stick.

I pushed my hands deep into my pockets, so I couldn't hold the Should Stick.

Time passed. I got used to keeping my hands in my pockets, and leaving the Should Stick at home.

There came a point when it felt safe to take my hands out of my pockets.

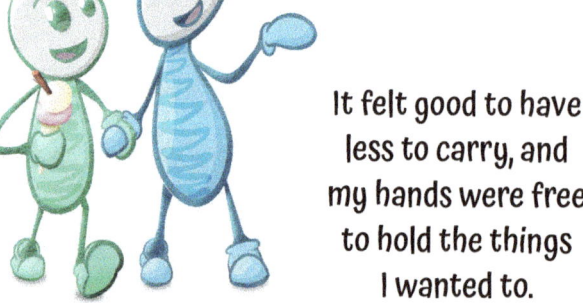

It felt good to have less to carry, and my hands were free to hold the things I wanted to.

I realised I hadn't poked anyone with a 'should' in ages.

I didn't want to do that anymore.

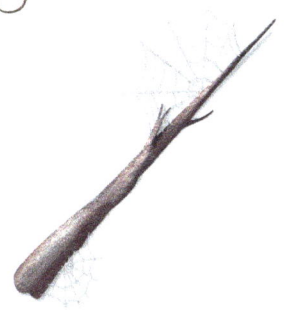

I put my Should Stick at the back of the cupboard, with all the other unwanted things, and closed the door.

But I wasn't free.

I still found myself thinking about the Should Stick.

When people poked me with their Should Sticks, I wanted to poke them back.

I doubted I would ever be free of it.

I pushed my hands back into my pockets.
I was determined not to pick up the
Should Stick ever again.

Deep in the bottom of the pocket,
I found something!

Hidden under the pocket fluff was
a button on a thin piece of string.

Engraved on the button were the words...

'Be Me'
'WARNING Self use only!!'

I hung the Be Me Button around my neck.

It looked perfect on me.

But nothing happened.

I showed the Be Me Button to others
(they wanted one too)
but still nothing happened.

I decided it must be broken.

But...

The Be Me Button was still pretty awesome to look at, so I wore it every day.

It went with everything I chose to wear. It was like it was made just for me!

Years went by.

And I hadn't thought about the Should Stick at all!

I'd changed and I hadn't noticed it happening.

That was when I realised what the Be Me Button was and how it worked!!

The Be Me Button protected me from the Should Stick.

When I was happy Being Me, I didn't need to prod and poke others.

And even better... Being Me protected me from everyone else's Should Sticks!

People would prod and poke, but I didn't feel it.

When I decided to 'Be Me', their Should Sticks couldn't hurt me.

I was so excited, I tried to give my
Be Me Button to my best friend,
but it didn't work.

That's the same as saying they **should**
have a Be Me Button, and I needed my
Should Stick to do that!

I realised everyone has to find
their **own** Be Me Button.

I'm so happy I found mine.

Because there really is only one **should** that matters, and that's the **should** that says...

"I should be **ME**."

The Should Stick

The End?

Part Two

What next?

I hope you enjoyed my story.

I wonder what thoughts and feelings it's prompted.

Maybe you're thinking about your own Should Stick.

Perhaps you're thinking about the prods and pokes you've felt from others.

Do you want to be free of your Should Stick, and from the prods and pokes of other people's Should Sticks?

Your own story starts with wanting to be you.

Where might your Be Me Button be hidden?

It might be small.

Maybe it's been hidden for a very long time, but if you want to find it, you will.

Now that you've found it, blow off the dust.

Hold it high and see it shine.

Put it on, hold it tight, say the words 'I want to Be Me' and... maybe... we can banish the Should Sticks forever.

The end of this book could be the beginning of your happy life.

On the following pages I offer you a simple exercise, to help you start your journey towards authenticity, and the freedom to be your unique self.

Part Three

How to Be Me – The Labels Exercise

The Labels Exercise

There are differing opinions on the helpfulness of 'labels'. When we use language as a means of communication and understanding, labels become inevitable. It's not the label that causes a problem, but our understanding of it and what it means for us.

Labels that represent our authenticity help us to understand ourselves and, when offered and explained, help others to understand us.

For example, one of my labels is 'reliable'. It's not the most exciting of labels but it is part of who I am and I like that aspect of me. When I offer that description to others, it helps them know a little more about me.

Many of my clients have found this exercise helpful and enlightening.

Here's a few thoughts from me to make the exercise easier.

1. This can be a powerful exercise, so take it steady and don't try to rush through it. Depending on your age, experiences and current challenges, you might have a lot of labels to work through, so think of this as a marathon not a sprint.
2. This is about you. There is no right or wrong, no good or bad. It's about finding what fits for you.
3. You can get someone to help you if you prefer. They need to support you in your process and not impose their own. Beware of 'shoulds' creeping in.
4. Be kind to yourself. Building self-awareness can raise aspects we'd rather not see. If this happens, accept these labels exist at present and maybe they are something to work on.
5. This is a start. This exercise is not the magic wand of authenticity. (I wish it was.) View it as the first step of the process towards becoming the real you.

Step 1

Write down, In the space provided, all the words and phrases that have been used to describe you in your life. These are your current labels. They can be your own. They can be labels given to you by others and can be from childhood or present day. They might include labels you like such as 'happy' or 'fun'. They might include labels you don't like, such as 'lazy' or 'selfish'.

Take your time. When you think you're finished, ask yourself a simple question; "Is there anything else?" and keep going until there isn't.

MY CURRENT LABELS

MY CURRENT LABELS

Step 2

Look at the labels you've collected. Give yourself a huge pat on the back and take a breath. Show yourself some empathy. Deep self-reflective work can be a challenging process.

On the next 3 pages you will see the following headings:

    IMPOSTER – **these are labels I want to be free of**

    AUTHENTIC – **these are labels I want to keep**

    EITHER/OR – **these are labels I'm not sure about**

Sort your labels from pages 58-59 into the three categories. Some might be easier to place than others, so take your time. You might find some additional labels show up as you do this. If so, add them to the relevant category.

IMPOSTER – these are labels I want to be free of

AUTHENTIC – these are labels I want to keep

EITHER/OR – these are labels I'm not sure about

Look at your three lists. Notice the size and shape of them.

Are there any themes?

What comes into your awareness?

What feelings are noticeable as you look at the lists?

Don't judge or criticise the lists or labels. Accept them for what they are and know that this is a big step towards being you.

Step 3

Next you will find an additional heading:

ASPIRATIONAL – **these are labels I want to gain**

These are new labels which are not on the previous lists. They represent qualities that you would like to gain and are aspects of your authentic self you have not allowed yourself to be.

This is a difficult section to do alone and can be easier with professional help, but if you sit with it for long enough some labels may come into your awareness. Maybe you have a deep desire to be 'funny', but no one has ever said that about you. Or maybe you want to put yourself first sometimes, but others have labelled this as 'selfish'. Instead of 'selfish' you might want a label that says 'self-care'. Place these labels on the Aspirational list.

Be bold. Remember there is no right or wrong. If there is a deep emotional connection which moves your hand to write something, then write it. You are building trust in your inner process and hidden labels will start to emerge.

ASPIRATIONAL – these are labels I want to gain

Step 4

Well done. You now have a great foundation to work from.

Now go back to your EITHER/OR list. The labels are on this list because you are uncertain about them. And that's OK. But now your aim is clarity. By the end of this step you want this list to be empty.

Over the next couple of pages you have an IMPOSTER list page and an AUTHENTIC list page. Look at every label on your EITHER/OR list and ask yourself this question for each one:

"If I had to move this label to the IMPOSTER list or the AUTHENTIC list, which would I choose?"

It's a binary choice. The label has to go somewhere. Remember, there is no right or wrong answer in this exercise. If you truly can't decide, then come back to the label later and see if your thoughts have changed. Look for evidence in your behaviours to support whether its authentic or an imposter. Check in with your feelings by imagining the label placed in either list. What emotion does this prompt? Does that suggest it's where you'd like it to be?

This part of the exercise is working on multiple levels. You are being curious and open, building and trusting your internal awareness, making decisions without fear of consequences and connecting with how you think, feel and behave.

Take your time over this step and it will enable you to really connect with your inner self.

Use the following 2 pages to complete your IMPOSTER and your AUTHENTIC lists.

FINAL IMPOSTER

FINAL AUTHENTIC

Step 5

If you've finished Step 4 you are back to three lists.

    IMPOSTER – **these are labels I want to be free of**

    AUTHENTIC – **these are labels I want to keep**

    ASPIRATIONAL – **these are labels I want to gain**

Time for more congratulations.

This is a really positive place to be.

You have greater clarity about who you are, who you don't want to be, and who you aspire to be.

Take a little time to read your lists and reflect on the process. Ask yourself the following question:

*"What was it like to focus on **ME**?"*

If this prompts any thoughts or feelings note them in the space below.

Step 6

You're nearing the end of the process and it's time to explore how you get from where you are, to where you want to be. Your work has resulted in clarity about what you want to leave behind, what you want to take with you and what you want to gain.

It's time to explore each list in turn.

YOUR IMPOSTER LABELS

These are the labels that you want to remove from your life. Removing them will require you to make changes. Some labels will be easier to remove than others whilst some will be 'sticky' and may take longer to work on.

It can be helpful to view these labels in the same way as you would a habit: with focus and determination you can change or even remove a long-standing habit. The same is true of labels. Exploring your behaviours is a great way to work with your labels.

Look at your IMPOSTER labels. Think about your behaviours and identify any of your current behaviours that support these labels.

These are the behaviours that keep the labels in place. Changing or stopping these behaviours will start to remove the label.

On the following pages write down the behaviours that keep your IMPOSTER labels in place. Reflect on each behaviour. Think about how you can stop them, reduce them, or even exchange them for a behaviour that is more supportive of your AUTHENTIC and ASPIRATIONAL labels.

IMPOSTER labels – behaviours I want to stop, reduce, exchange

IMPOSTER labels – behaviours I want to stop, reduce, exchange

Your AUTHENTIC labels

These are the labels that will continue to be part of your life. Exploring your behaviours also works well with reinforcing AUTHENTIC labels.

Look at your AUTHENTIC labels. Think about your behaviours and identify any of your current behaviours that support these labels.

These are the behaviours that keep the labels in place. Keeping or enhancing these behaviours will retain and reinforce these labels.

On the following pages write down the behaviours that keep your AUTHENTIC labels in place. Reflect on each behaviour. Think about how you can reinforce them, increase them or find even more supportive behaviours for these labels.

- **Maximise this list.**
- **Absolutely go for it.**
- **These are your strengths.**

These behaviours are familiar and known to you and others. You already accept these labels and know they are right for you, so make them count and feel that authenticity grow.

AUTHENTIC labels ~ behaviours I want to reinforce, increase, support

AUTHENTIC labels – behaviours I want to reinforce, increase, support

Your ASPIRATIONAL labels

Some of these labels may feel new and scary. That's understandable as this is where you break free of the 'shoulds' of your life and become the person you were born to be. Once again, you can explore the new behaviours you need to adopt to achieve your ASPIRATIONAL self.

Think about the behaviours that would reflect these labels; be curious and open about what they might look like. Maybe you know a role model or a fictional character who behaves in this way and you can emulate what they do. In time you will find your own authentic route, but to start off with, emulating an aspirational behaviour is a great way of trying it on for size.

On the following pages, write down behaviours that will develop your ASPIRATIONAL labels. Reflect on each behaviour. Think about how you can find them, practice them, and build them into new habits.

ASPIRATIONAL labels – behaviours I want to find, practice, build

ASPIRATIONAL labels – behaviours I want to find, practice, build

Step 7

A WORD OF WISDOM

This whole process can take weeks, months, even years to work on. Working on authenticity is the most important job you will ever have. It's your life's work. If, like me, you're a little older and have lots of labels, don't despair. When you focus on your AUTHENTIC and ASPIRATIONAL labels it's amazing how many labels on your IMPOSTER list start to drop off.

We only have so much room for labels and AUTHENTICITY leaves no room for IMPOSTERS.

A final word from my own experience. I started with a long list of labels which have become more refined over time. Some have dropped off. New ones have arrived and some are now so firmly embedded they are a part of me that no one else can change.

Good luck with your journey. It's time to Be You.

Challenges along the way and how to manage them

Human beings can be slow to change, even when it's something we want. Here you'll find three of the most common issues that might get in the way of your progress.

INNER CRITIC/SABOTEUR

At various points in the process your inner critic or saboteur might appear. This voice might be familiar to you, it might be quite loud and insistent, and it needs attending to. It is most likely to appear when you start to look at changing behaviours in Step 5. This voice will use phrases like:

'I can't stop doing that.'

'Others won't let me change that.'

'I've been doing this my whole life; I can't change now.'

'I've tried this before; nothing will ever work.'

'I can't do that, I'll be embarrassed.'

'If I try that, I'll fail.'

The first thing to understand is that the intention of this voice is to keep you safe: it means well. It is however working from a flawed concept. The simple concept which drives an inner critic is:

SAME = SAFE   DIFFERENT = DANGER

This is the one simple message which underlies many psychological issues such as anxiety, low self-worth, confidence and many others. It's part of our primal survival response which views anything new and different as potentially life threatening. It is therefore an extremely powerful voice and will resist being told to be quiet, as its aim is to keep you alive.

This message has to be challenged in a very specific way or it just gets louder and more insistent.

First. Accept that it's an emotional voice and it means well. It's a fearful voice which is trying to keep us safe.

Second. An emotional voice needs an emotional response before we can engage a rational thinking process.

Third. The message is not true. It's an absolute message which translates emotionally as:

SAME = ALWAYS SAFE   DIFFERENT = ALWAYS DANGER

You work with this voice by offering one very simple thing – **REASSURANCE**.

We counter the words of an inner critic with reassuring words of our own.

'I'll never be able to do that,' becomes

'This feels dangerous. I'm feeling scared. I feel like I might fail. And that's all ok and understandable. I'm doing something very different and that makes it feel dangerous. I know that different doesn't always mean danger and that staying the same isn't where I want to be. I wonder how I might feel if I keep going? I wonder if I can create a different behaviour which will feel safe in time?'

See how the emotional response is accepted not denied. The message of 'different = danger' is named and challenged. There is an acknowledgement that you want to be someone different and a sense that if you keep going then different will start to feel safe; it might even start to feel familiar.

Changing short statements, which are designed to stop your progress, into a reassuring and questioning inner dialogue keeps you moving forward. Practice with your own words and your own phrases.

There is a further crucial aspect to working with an inner critical voice. We have to play it at its own game and use – **REPETITION**.

A critical voice sustains itself by repetition. This is why you might find yourself thinking the same things over and over again until you finally give in. At this point the inner critic is satisfied that it's kept you safe and it can wait until it's needed again.

Your reassuring words therefore need to be repeated. Repeated as often, and more than, the words of the critic. We beat an inner critic with **REPEATED REASSURANCE**.

You might even create a mantra; a simple reassuring phrase which you can repeat when doubt creeps in.

EXTERNAL CRITICS AND SABOTEURS

Beware of external critics and saboteurs. You may have people in your life who like you just as you are. Maybe you meet their needs, if not your own. Maybe their view of life is not helpful for you. They might be very active in sticking labels on you. Ones that you no longer wish to keep.

This offers a challenge as you work through your authenticity process. You might successfully remove a label, only to find that someone else will try to stick it back on. That someone will prod you with their own Should Stick labelled 'you should still be like that'.

This will happen. It's normal and they usually do it from innocence and ignorance.

The technique for success is to remove the label, explain that you no longer want to be like this and you don't accept the label anymore. Those who care about you will listen and understand and try not to give you the label again. Others might keep prodding to keep the label firmly attached. You may have a decision to make about whether they are people you want in your new authentic life.

The same issue might occur for your aspirational labels. Some people around you might find these new behaviours scary and challenging. They might try a range of techniques to stop you doing something new; being someone new. Common techniques can include:

- **Mockery** – shaming you for the new behaviour
- **Criticism** – shaming you for the new behaviour
- **Alternative suggestions** – shaming you for the new behaviour
- **Gossiping** – shaming you for the new behaviour
- **Ignoring you** – shaming you for the new behaviour

I think you get the idea. Anything anyone does, which isn't supportive of the changes you are trying to make, will generally result in a shame response. That sense that you're doing something wrong and others are judging you for it. This may not be their intention but it is generally how it feels.

I suggest you use the same technique as described earlier and explain that this is a new aspect of you and it's here to stay. If they try to remove the label, you'll just stick it back on.

You can't control whether people will like your new authentic self. The most important thing is that YOU like your new authentic self.

FEELING STUCK AND SEEKING HELP

Sometimes we get stuck. Deep reflective processes are challenging and we can end up in a loop where we keep returning to the same place. It's at these points we might benefit from some safe external help with our reflection.

If you need help to work on you, find a coach who specialises in authenticity. They don't have to support you through the whole process and it can be really effective to get help just for those times when you're a bit stuck.

One word of warning. There is no quick fix. No one can give you that. So beware of anyone who says they can help you become your authentic self in a few short (and often expensive) sessions. Authenticity, by its very nature, is about self-reflection, self-awareness and building self-care practices that sustain you.

This process may take some time. But remember; AUTHENTICITY is already in YOU. You might just need a little help now and again because it's been hiding for such long time.

Acknowledgements and thanks

Alison Miller for being there when the concept first popped into my head, and for your feedback on my early version.

Vicky Hughes and Helen McCabe for your thoughts and reflections on my early version.

Maria Iliffe-Wood for your awesome support help and guidance. This wouldn't have happened without you.

Steve Pitcher for pulling the words and the pictures together.

...and Matt Roberts because you brought this to life and added so much to the process. I think you understand this book almost as much as I do.

About Tracey Hartshorn

After a thirty-year career in the public sector, Tracey left the world of finance and management to follow her ambition to support people to achieve authenticity. She now works as a coach and psychotherapist in independent practice, based in the UK. She is accredited with the British Association for Counselling and Psychotherapy and is passionate about working from a firm ethical and theoretical base.

Tracey is a great believer in psycho-education: the provision of information and knowledge to help clients understand how they think, feel and behave. If knowledge is power, then the process of sharing this empowers us all.

Tracey's aspiration is to help others to achieve a life free of the constraints of external messages and conditions. A life which offers real awareness and choice; awareness of who you are and choice about what you do.

Tracey aspires to have a writing shed in the garden and to spend far too much time in there.

🌐 www.traceyhartshorn.co.uk

📷 @beproudbetruebeyou

🐦 @Tracey_Coaching

About Matt Roberts

Matt was a professional musician who studied trumpet at the Royal Birmingham Conservatoire of Music. Due to the uncertain nature of the world in 2019, he took the opportunity to pursue his other love; illustration.

Over this short period, Matt has undertaken projects which have turned NHS staff into superheroes; designed a series of five twenty-foot murals; created promotional artwork for the Nottingham Albert Hall; collaborated with artists from around the world to create a calendar, to raise money for the fight against Motor Neurone Disease. He continues to work with clients on both personal and professional commissions.

Matt runs drawing challenges on his rapidly growing Instagram account and teaches classes, both online and in person, on how to get started with drawing and the positive effects art has on your wellbeing.

@Mattdrawsstuffuk

@Mattdrawsstuffuk

www.ingramcontent.com/pod-product-compliance
Lightning Source LLC
Chambersburg PA
CBHW041147110526
44590CB00027B/4158